THE
AWESOME
EGYPTIANS
ACTIVITY
BOOK

Terry Deary ✵ Martin Brown

■SCHOLASTIC

WHAT IS AN AWESOME EGYPTIAN?

The awesome Egyptians weren't just fabulous pharaohs and mean mummies!
Ninety per cent of ancient Egyptians were peasants who worked very hard.
Peasants were like property – if a pharaoh gave land to a nobleman then
the peasants were thrown in as well.

*There were few slaves in Egypt, but if you were a peasant you may as
well have been one! Peasants were counted along with the cattle to show
how rich a landowner was. Women were not counted because they were
not worth as much as cattle!*

Below are the peasants and cattle that work on Ali Fayed's land.
Can you find them in the picture above and work out how rich he is?

TOTAL

When the Nile was in flood, peasants were ordered to work on the pyramids. If you didn't work fast enough then you would be punished by whipping or by having bits chopped off your body – a finger or a toe, perhaps. Follow the paths to work out which peasant is going to face the chop.

Some peasants who worked hard on the pyramids suffered terrible conditions. Unscramble the words in CAPITAL LETTERS to find out what happened.

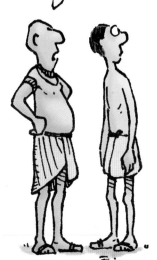

1) Workers dragged huge TESON KLOCBS for 60 kilometres over the GRINNUB RESTED.

2) They were paid with some REDAB, linen and MINTTONE.

3) At the end of the day, workers trudged back to their barracks – rough MELONSITE shelters with DUM SOFORL.

4) Rooms were ROCWDDE with no TREWA or LOITETS.

5) The barracks really KNUTS from human GASWEE and from the MANALIS that shared the space.

6) The workers wanted to go home but they knew they would die of NOTATRAVIS before they got there!

THESE CONDITIONS ARE NOT FIT FOR A PEASANT

WRITE LIKE AN EGYPTIAN

To be a top man in Egypt you had to be able to read and write. Boys (not girls) had to go to school in the temple and suffer under terrible teachers who worked them and beat them without mercy. One tough teacher said that boys needed a good beating if they were going to learn. In Egypt you had to suffer to succeed.

Egyptian writing is called hieroglyphics. Sometimes a hieroglyphic sign means a letter – the way it does in our alphabet. Sometimes it means a whole word. Hieroglyphs were deliberately complicated so that it took a long time to read and write them. It meant that those who could read and write were more important.

A. vulture
B. leg
D. hand
F. viper
G. pot or stand
CH. rope
I. reed
J. serpent
K. basket
L. lion

M. owl
N. water
P. stool
Q. hill
R. mouth
S. cloth
T. loaf
W. chick
Y. reeds
Z. bolt

Here are some Egyptian hieroglyphs. Use them to write your name. The Egyptians didn't have signs for letters C, E, O, U, and X, so you will need to add these letters with the hieroglyphs

FISH, HAND, SQUIGGLE SPELLS CAT

See if you can read these two messages. The sound of the letters is more important than the spelling. Anyway, who says the Egyptians had to be good at spelling? Are you?

EH?

4

If you think school is bad in the 21st century, you should have gone to school in ancient Egypt. Learning to be a scribe was hard. The teachers were stern and the discipline was strict. Unscramble the words in CAPITAL LETTERS to read this text called 'Advice to a Young Scribe'…

O scribe do not be LIED, or you shall be CRUDES.

Do TON give your EARTH to RULES PEA or you HALLS fail. Do not PENDS a day in SEEN LIDS or you shall be AT BEEN. A YOB'S ear is on his DICE BASK and he listens HEWN he is BEE TAN!

Can you find the list of these hieroglyphs hidden in the grid below? They can be found written up, down, backwards and across. Then try and work out what the hieroglyphs say. If you can, you are on the way to becoming an awesome Egyptian expert!

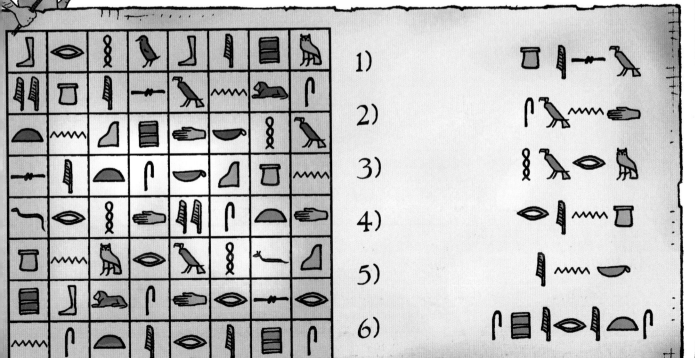

1)

2)

3)

4)

5)

6)

GRUESOME GODS

Egyptians wanted to reach the spirit world that the priests taught about. There was an awesome number of gods for an Egyptian to please before he or she got there. And if they annoyed one, well, it was tombs-full of trouble for them!

Egyptian gods were unbelievably old. They had lived before people existed and now treated humans as if they were a mixture of toys and servants. The gods controlled the world and everything that happened. They demanded respect. Can you match the images of the gods below to their descriptions?

1) Anubis – the jackal-headed god of the dead. He helped to prepare mummies.

2) Bes – the dwarf god of happiness, and protector of the family.

3) Hathor – the cow-horned goddess of love. She also looked after happiness, dancing and music.

4) Horus – the falcon-headed god who looked after the pharaoh.

5) Isis – wife of Osiris. She took special care of women and children.

6) Osiris – god of death and rebirth, the Underworld and the Earth. Long ago he had taught people to farm.

7) Ptah – the god who spoke the names of all the things in the world. By doing this he made them exist.

8) Re – the Sun God. Some said he had made people. The Egyptians called themselves, 'the cattle of Re'.

9) Seth – god of the desert and storms. The enemy of Osiris.

10) Sekhmet – the lioness goddess of war.

11) Sobek – the crocodile-headed god. He controlled water supplies.

12) Thoth – the ibis-headed god of wisdom who invented speaking and writing.

Need an awesome answer to a powerful problem? Read the Dear God… letters below and use the list of gods on page 6 to work out which god each person is praying to.

1) Oh great _Sobek_. My land is short of water and my crops are dying.

2) Mighty _Hathor_. My youngest son died of fever three months ago. Since then my wife is heart-broken. Please help her to enjoy life again.

3) Oh wise _Thoth_. My son wishes to be a scribe, but he is so bad at learning his hieroglyphs that his teachers are threatening to throw him out of school. Beatings don't seem to help.

4) Please give me strength, oh vengeful _Sekhmet_. Raiders from the Red Land have attacked our village. Help us to defeat them.

5) Please, sweet _Hathor_. I am madly in love with the most beautiful girl, but she laughs at my dancing. I am terribly clumsy and fall over my own feet.

ERRR!

GO ON! DO YOU WANT TO DANCE WITH HER OR DON'T YOU!?

Most awesome Egyptian myths have various versions of the same story. Here is one version of the Isis and Osiris story. Sadly our suffering scribe has scrambled the terrible tale in places. Can you unscramble the words in CAPITAL LETTERS?

Osiris was an awesome king. He was loved by his loyal wife, Isis, and all of his people. Only Osiris's brother, Set, hated him. He was LASOUJE of his brother and planned to kill him.

Set DOINGEARS a large feast. At the height of the festivities, Set produced a casket and ACNDOENUN that it would be given to whoever it fitted. All the guests tried the casket for size, but none fitted, until finally, Osiris stepped into the casket. Set slammed the lid closed and sealed the casket shut with boiling lead. The SALDEE coffin was then thrown into the Nile.

Isis SEHCRAED for the casket all over Egypt. At last, she found it where it had come to rest in the roots of a huge tree.

Isis took the coffin back for a proper ALIRUB. For safety, she hid it in the marshes beside the Nile. Sneaky Set found the casket and was so GEDENRA he chopped the body of Osiris into pieces, and RECAEDSTT the parts throughout the land of Egypt.

Poor Isis set out again looking for the bits of her husband. At last, she found all the parts except one (his naughty bit) and reassembled Osiris and PAREDPW him in bandages. The first mummy!

Osiris was also a daddy and his son, Horus, went out to battle his savage uncle Set. After a series of battles, neither was able to win. In the end, Osiris was made king of the underworld, Horus – king of the living and Set – ruler of the deserts as the god of evil. So they all died happily ever after!

PHASCINATING PHARAOHS

After the Egyptians invented gods, some clever people said, 'Actually, we are those gods you pray to! So give us food, build us palaces, worship us and we'll look after you.' These clever people became known as 'pharaohs' – probably because they had a 'fair-old' life with peasants 'slaving' for them!

Pharaohs ruled for almost 3,000 years so there were bound to be a few odd ones among all that lot. If there had been newspapers in those days then imagine the headlines. But there weren't and even if there had been, they'd have been crumbly by now and key words may have fallen out. Can you add the missing words to these headlines?

Missing words, but not in the correct order:
Greek, hundred, money, goose, murder, elephants, magician, lion, woman, wrinkly.

1 SENSATION! PHARAOH HATSHEPSUT IS A _____

2 HORROR! IS TUTANKHAMUN A VICTIM OF *Murder*?

3 SHOCK! TUT'S WIDOW, ANKHESENAMUN, MARRIES A _____!

4 ASTONISHING! PEPY II HITS A _____!

5 WONDER! HAIR CLIP FOUND BY _____!

6 AMAZING! PHARAOH'S ENTERTAINER PUTS HEAD BACK ON _____!

7 ASTOUNDING! RAMESES II FACES ENEMY ARMY WITH JUST A *Lion* !

8 WOW! THUTMOSE III ESCAPES BEING KILLED BY *elephants*

I WOULDN'T LOOK UP THERE IF I WERE YOU

9 DESPICABLE! PSAMMETICHUS HOLDS OFF INVASION WITH _____!

10 EGYPTIAN SHAME! CLEOPATRA IS A _____!

After ruling for 30 years, the pharaoh had to prove his fitness by running round a fixed course. This terrible trial was held at the Heb-sed festival. Can you work out which obstacle course will lead the pharaoh to the finish line?

The carvings on all Egyptian monuments show the king as a conqueror. What if you lost? Don't worry, the scribes can still say you won! Rameses II fought the Hittites at the Battle of Qadesh in Syria. The Egyptian scribes described his victory. The Hittite scribes described the same battle – but in the Hittite story the Hittites won! Look at the two battle scenes below. Spot ten differences between the two and circle them with a pencil.

POWERFUL PYRAMIDS

Pharaohs were no different to other Egyptians. They also worried about reaching the spirit world when they died. They had huge stone tombs built. These were called pyramids. When the pharaohs died, their bodies would be safe inside a burial chamber. The pyramid contained everything the pharaoh would need in the afterlife … including a toilet.

> *There are some awesome things you ought to know about the pyramids. Here is a crossword with a difference – it doesn't have any clues. The words missing from the facts below make up the answers. The information in brackets tells you where they should go in the grid.*

1) A pyramid was supposedly built as a huge stone _____ (6 across, 4 letters) of a pharaoh.

2) The burial chamber in the centre was filled with awesome _____ (5 down, 6 letters) for the pharaoh to take into the afterlife.

3) The riches were a temptation to _____ (4 across, 7 letters). The pyramid builders tried to fool the thieves by making false doors, staircases and corridors.

4) The base of the Great Pyramid of Cheops is equal to the area of seven or eight _____ (3 down, 8 letters) pitches (230 metres x 230 metres).

5) The pyramids are close to the _____ (1 down, 4 letters) because some of the huge stones had to be carried from the quarries by boat.

6) The pyramids are all on the west bank of the Nile – the side on which the ___ (7 across, 3 letters) sets. This is for religious reasons.

7) The pyramids were built from enormous stone blocks. But how did the Egyptians _____ (2 across, 4 letters) them when they had no cranes?

Not everyone agrees the pyramids are graves, of course. Thinking about those great lumps of dense stone, are people with great lumps of dense brains who have other ideas. But which of the following wacky ideas have some people seriously believed? Answer true or false...

Someone has said that the pyramids are...

1) Adverts. The priests wanted to leave something to show the world how great they were.

2) Simple landmarks. All maps would be drawn with the pyramids at the centre and distances worked out from there.

3) Chambers of horrors. Dead kings were stuck inside, then the Egyptian people were charged two onions an hour to walk around and view their kingly corpses.

4) Sundials. The shadow from the Great Pyramid would be used to work out the time.

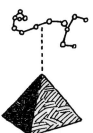

5) Mathematical horoscopes. They've been used to predict the birth of Christ, the date of World War 1 and the end of the world – AD 2979 if you're worried.

6) Star calculators. They help to measure the speed of light, the distance from the earth to the sun and to keep a record of the movement of the stars.

7) Calendars. They can measure the length of a year to three decimal points.

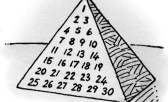

8) The Great Pyramid is an observatory for watching and recording the movements of the stars.

9) Centres of invisible forces of the Universe. Weird things can happen there – like blunt razors turning sharp and people feeling wobbly at the knees when they enter.

10) Maths calculators. Take the distance around the edges and the angles and whatnot and you can work out the distance round a circle (its circumference) if you know the distance across the diameter.

The biggest pyramid is the Pyramid of Cheops – known to this day as The Great Pyramid. How many times can you spot the word PYRAMID in the grid? The words may run across, up, down, diagonally, forwards or backwards.

P	I	M	A	R	Y	P	Y	R	A	M	I	D
Y	D	I	M	P	Y	R	A	M	I	D	I	I
R	M	P	Y	R	A	M	I	D	Y	M	P	M
A	I	M	A	Y	P	I	M	I	P	I	Y	A
M	P	M	P	R	Y	D	I	M	P	M	P	R
I	I	Y	R	A	M	P	Y	R	P	M	R	Y
D	P	A	R	Y	D	D	I	M	A	R	Y	P

POTTY PYRAMIDS

Pyramids are H-U-G-E! The Great Pyramid in Giza is made up of about 2,300,000 stone blocks. If you broke the Great Pyramid into slabs 30cm thick, you could build a wall 1 metre high that would stretch all the way around France. If you had a little more time, you could cut the stone into rods about 6cm square – join them together and you'd have enough to reach the Moon!

Can you find the words listed in the pyramids? The words can be found written up, down, backwards and across. Then unscramble the letters in the mini pyramid to work out which civilization lived 5,000 years ago!

CAT
CHAMBER
CURSE
DESERT
EGYPT
EMBALM
GODS
GRAVE

MUMMY
NILE
PHARAOH
~~PRIEST~~
PYRAMID

ROBBER
SAND
SCRIBE
SPIRITS

SUN
TOMB
TREASURE

The

_ _ _ _ _ _ _ _ _ _

I WOULDN'T BE SEEN DEAD IN ONE OF THOSE THINGS

DAILY BLAH
(7 January 1993)

BINGO

STOP PRESS: News Flash

Archaeologists in Egypt have found the ruins of a small pyramid, a few metres from the Great Pyramid of Cheops at Giza. It was discovered by chance during a cleaning operation. This brings the number of known pyramids to 96. Can you count how many overlapping pyramids there are here?

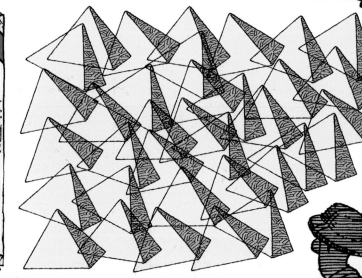

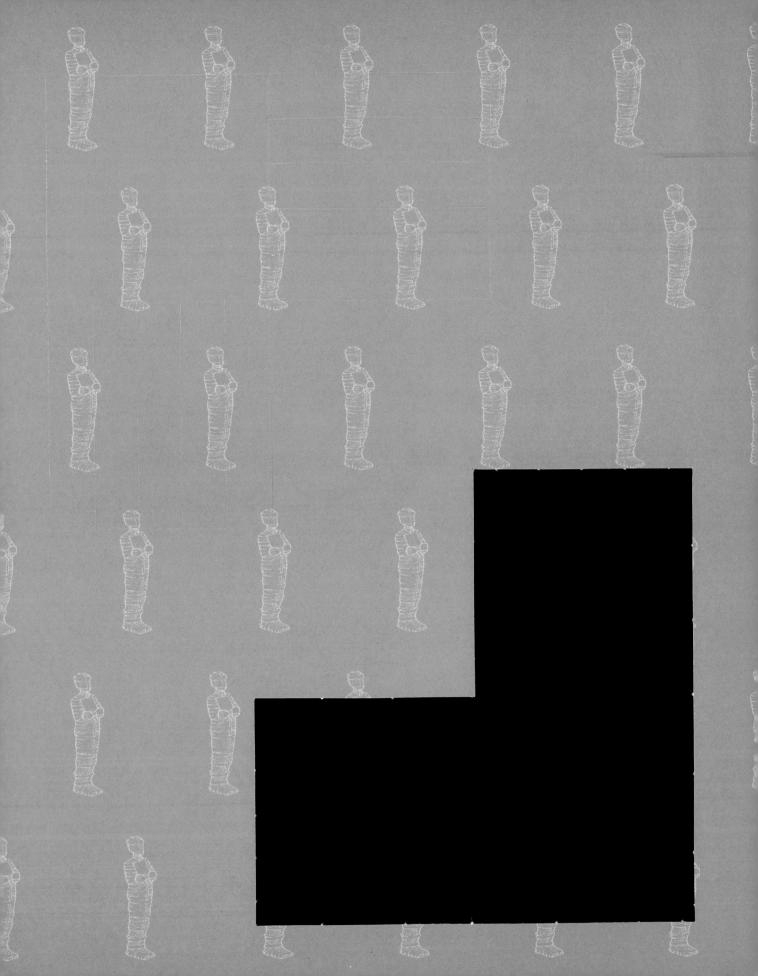

Here are two potty picture puzzles that are sure to get you in a flap!

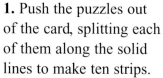

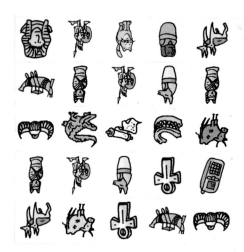

Fold all ten strips to leave twenty-five things you might find in a pharaoh's tomb.

1. Push the puzzles out of the card, splitting each of them along the solid lines to make ten strips.

2. Weave and fold the strips inwards, along the dotted lines, to solve each puzzle.

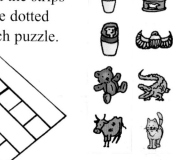

Do you think you are clever enough to do this one again? This time, fold all ten strips to show the five mummies that the body bits belong to.

Do you think you could be an artist? Here's your chance to prove yourself.
A pharaoh has a new pyramid that needs to be decorated with the picture below.
Copy the lines in each square onto the empty grid. Then colour your picture in.

Remember the Egyptian style. Heads are painted sideways, but the eye is shown full face. Legs are shown sideways and both shoulders should be in view. The more important the person, the bigger they are. Pharaoh gets most space.

If you work with some friends you could copy the drawing and make a wall painting. DANGER – don't use the living room wall without first asking … or you could be history.

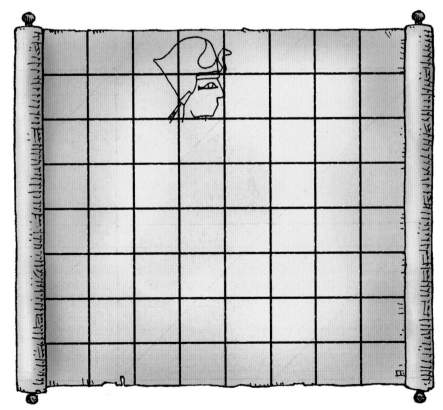

13

MAGICAL MUMMIES

Egyptians believed that one day the world would end. When it does, then everyone who has a body will move on to a wonderful afterlife. But if your body rots, you will miss out on this treat. So it was the Egyptians' duty to make sure their dead pharaohs didn't rot. They turned them into mummies.

The men who made dead bodies into mummies were called embalmers. They took the bodies to a place called the Beautiful House to work on them. Here's how to make a mummy. Unfortunately the instructions have been mixed up by a mummy's curse. Can you put them back in the right order?

A) Rip open the front of the body and take out the liver, the stomach, the intestines and the lungs – but leave the heart inside.

B) Throw the brain away and pack the skull with 'natron' – a sort of salt that stops bodies rotting.

C) Stuff the empty body with rags to give it the right shape, then sew it up.

D) Take the body to a Beautiful House – that's an open-ended tent in the open air – so the disgusting smells are blown away!

E) Wash the liver, the stomach, the intestines and the lungs in wine and place them in their sealed canopic jars.

F) Put the body on a wooden table with bars of wood (not a solid top) so you can reach underneath to bandage it.

G) Perform the ceremony of the 'Opening of the mouth' – or the mummy won't be able to eat, drink or speak in the next life!

H) Soak the body in natron for 70 days till it is well pickled.

I) Wrap the body in bandages from head to foot.

J) Remove the brain by pushing a chisel up the nose to break through, then hook the brain out with a piece of wire.

The following mummies will tell you a bit of mummy magic. Some of them are not telling the truth – can you work out which ones are?

1. IF A BIT FALLS OFF MY BODY, EMBALMERS WILL REPLACE IT WITH A LUMP OF WOOD

2. I WAS BURIED WITH A SCROLL OF MAGIC SPELLS CALLED 'THE BOOK OF THE DEAD'

3. THE LAST MUMMY WAS MADE IN 55BC

4. PEOPLE IN BRITAIN WATCHED MUMMIES BEING UNWRAPPED FOR FUN

MUMMIES MAKE GOOD FUEL FOR FIRE

5. EGYPTIANS BELIEVED THAT MUMMIES PASSED THROUGH A DANGEROUS PLACE FULL OF MONSTERS

6. BRITISH PEOPLE KEPT MUMMIES FOR DECORATION

Intestines can be pretty messy, so it's best to tidy them into a special container. The Egyptians made theirs out of clay. You can make one from a drinks bottle.

To make a canopic jar, you will need:
- An empty plastic drinks bottle
- Paints or felt-tip pens or pencils
- Modelling clay
- Drawing paper
- Sticky tape or glue
- Sand or pebbles

1) Take the top off the drinks bottle and rinse it out.
2) Put some sand or pebbles in the bottle to stop it falling over.
3) Decorate the paper with hieroglyphs and Egyptian pictures and symbols.

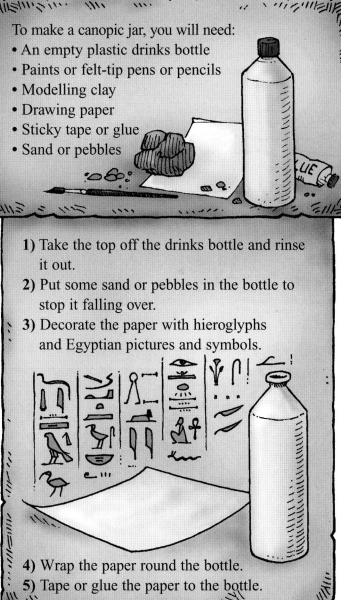

4) Wrap the paper round the bottle.
5) Tape or glue the paper to the bottle.

I THINK WE'LL NEED A BIGGER CANOPIC JAR

6) Use the modelling clay to make a lid. Make the lid into the shape of one of the four Sons of Horus.

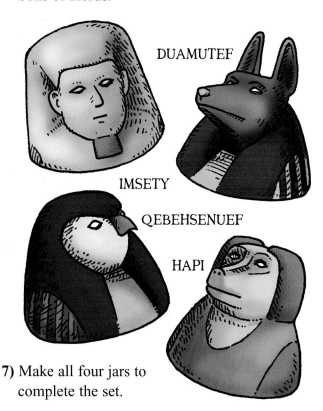

DUAMUTEF

IMSETY

QEBEHSENUEF

HAPI

7) Make all four jars to complete the set.

The Egyptians were very superstitious. They also believed in lucky charms. Here is one you could make for yourself out of card to wear around your neck. The three symbols are Egyptian hieroglyphic signs for three words…

'all'   'life'   'protection'

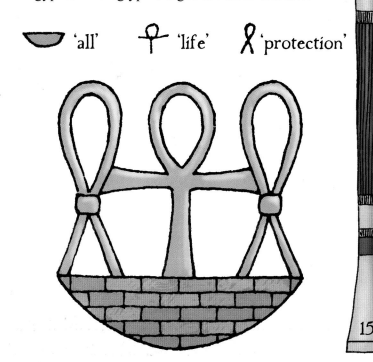

15

FATE OF THE MUMMY

After the pharaoh was turned into a mummy, they would be placed in a coffin in a tomb which was sealed. This was to shut out the grave-robbers. The dead person would then have to pass through a dangerous place known as the Duat. The dangers were monsters, boiling lakes and rivers of fire. The snake that spat poison was particularly nasty.

The monsters that live in the Duat could be overcome with the right spells. The spells were written down on Egyptian paper (papyrus) and left near the coffin. This is the 'Book of the Dead.' Can you help the dead pharaoh find his way through the Duat to the gates of Yaru (the Egyptian afterlife)?

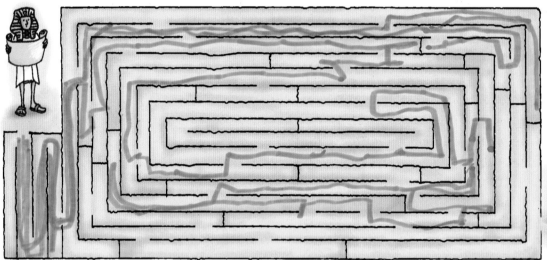

At the gates of Yaru, the pharaoh's heart was placed in one side of a balance and in the other side was the Feather of Truth (this held all the lies of your past life). If the heart was lighter than the feather, the dead person was allowed through the gates. But if it was heavier … their heart was eaten by the Devourer. Colour in the dotted areas to find out what this terrifying monster looked like.

COULDN'T YOU GET A SMALLER FEATHER?

The Egyptians mummified more than their pharaohs. They mummified the pharaohs' pets and buried them in the pyramids to keep the dead kings company in the afterlife.
Look at these two pictures. Spot ten differences between the two and circle them with a pencil.

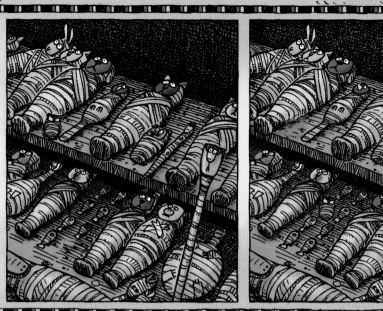

Pilgrims came to ancient Egypt like holiday-makers to Blackpool. They bought miniature mummies as souvenirs. To find out exactly what the Egyptians bought, answer all 5 questions below. Use your answers to work your way around the puzzle. You should only make words from letters that are next to each other. The letters that remain will give you the answer.

1) A magician pulls this long-eared creature out of a hat: _ _ _ _ _ _ (6)

2) When you're looking for a compliment you are said to be _ _ _ _ing for one. (4)

3) Man's best friend: _ _ _ (3)

4) If your bedroom's in a mess, your mum would call it a _ _ _sty! (3)

5) When you go under a very low bridge you should _ _ _ _ to avoid hitting your head. (4)

START

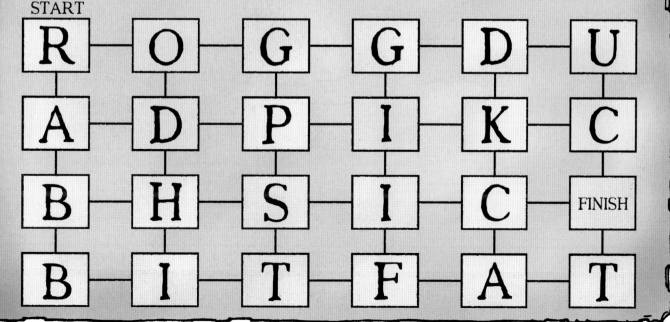

17

GRUESOME GRAVE-ROBBERS

Pyramids were filled with goodies so the pharaohs would be as rich in the next life as they were in this life. Of course they've all been robbed now – some were robbed at the time of the burial and the rest have been cleaned out by greedy treasure hunters in the twentieth century.

Pharaohs eventually realised that a pyramid was a huge stone advert saying, "Look at my grave! Look at my wealth!" The only answer was to hide the tombs. The pharaohs switched to being buried in hidden caves in the rocks. Help this grave-robber find the correct path that leads to the pharaoh's treasure.

START

FINISH

Cast yourself back in time a few thousand years. You are travelling through ancient Egypt and you've run out of copper coins. You want to rob a pyramid or a rock tomb (and get away with it). Answer Yes or No to the questions below and turn to page 24 to see if you have what it takes to become a successful grave-robber.

1) Do you do all the work yourself so that you get to keep all the loot?

2) Will you have to spend money to get people on your side?

3) Is it a good idea to go through the front entrance of the pyramid?

4) Should you bribe everyone concerned with the burial?

5) Is setting fire to the tomb a good idea?

6) As a grave-robber, should you avoid travelling merchants?

7) Should you spend your treasure so there's no evidence that it was you?

8) Is it easy to find your way around the inside of a pyramid?

9) Should you try to steal the body before it is buried?

10) Will you be punished if you get caught?

Many tomb-builders became grave-robbers. They grew hungry when their wages were late. They tried going on strike and marching on the officials' houses with chants of, "We are hungry! We are hungry!" When that failed they turned to robbing the tombs they'd helped to build. Look at the two scenes below. Spot eight differences between the two and circle them with a pencil.

CURIOUS CURSES

Mummies are a bit creepy. Looking at corpses of long-dead people is enough to give you goose-bumps on your goose-bumps! But it's not creepy enough for some people. They imagine the mummies aren't just shrivelled flesh – they believe the mummy spirits wander around. These spirits bring curses and spells to the living people who disturb their rest and rob their graves.

Lots of 'true' mummy stories have been told over the past century. This is one of them – see if you believe it! Count Louis Hamon wrote to his friend, Lord Carnarvon. He begged him to be careful on his expedition in Egypt. Put the pictures in the right order to find out why Louis Hamon wanted to warn his friend.

G — 1375 BC... KING AKHNATON ARGUED WITH HIS DAUGHTER
TAKE HER AWAY... EXECUTE HER!

C — THEN LOCK IT IN THE SAFE AND LET'S FORGET ABOUT IT...

J — A SUDDEN WIND TORE OPEN THE DOOR... THE HAMONS FELL TO THE FLOOR AND AN EGYPTIAN WOMAN APPEARED

I — HAMON'S WIFE HATED IT ON SIGHT...
CAN'T YOU GIVE IT TO A MUSEUM?
I'VE TRIED – THEY ALL REFUSE

D — BUT AS HE CLOSED THE BOOK, THE HOUSE WAS PLUNGED INTO DARKNESS... A BLAST SHOOK THE HOUSE

F — BUT IN OCTOBER 1922 THE HAMONS OPENED THE SAFE. THEY STOOD BACK IN HORROR...
IT'S NOT MUMMIFIED. IT'S AS SOFT AND FRESH AS MINE

E — THE HAND
GONE!

L — DESTROY IT!
NO, SHE DESERVES A DECENT FUNERAL

N — AND ON 31 OCTOBER, HALLOWE'EN, HAMON READ PRAYERS FROM AN ANCIENT "BOOK OF THE DEAD"

A — BUT HE WASN'T SATISFIED WITH HER DEATH
CUT OFF HER HAND! WITHOUT A COMPLETE BODY SHE WILL NOT ENTER THE AFTERLIFE

H — THE GRISLY RELIC, THE HAND, WAS PASSED DOWN THROUGH ARAB FAMILIES, TILL THIS CENTURY, IT REACHED A SHEIK
YOU HAVE CURED ME OF MALARIA, HAMON, LET ME GIVE YOU A GIFT

B — AND THE SHEIK GAVE HAMON THE PRINCESS'S HAND
I COULDN'T ACCEPT SUCH A... A PRECIOUS GIFT...
I INSIST!

O — THE FIGURE BENT OVER THE HAND AND VANISHED

M — SO THE PRINCESS WAS BURIED... BUT HER HAND WAS NOT

K — LOOK! SHE HAS NO HAND!

Fill in the grid below with the correct sequence.

| G | | | | | | | C | | | | | | |

Lord Carnarvon ignored his friend's letter. His expedition found the fabulous tomb of Tutankhamun and seven weeks after that, Lord Carnarvon was dead! He got a mosquito bite on his left cheek which became infected. When doctors examined Tutankhamun's mummy, they noticed a strange mark – on his left cheek!
Copy the picture boxes into the grid to see the full picture.

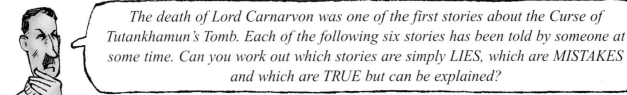

The death of Lord Carnarvon was one of the first stories about the Curse of Tutankhamun's Tomb. Each of the following six stories has been told by someone at some time. Can you work out which stories are simply LIES, which are MISTAKES and which are TRUE but can be explained?

1) Arthur Mace was one of the first to enter the tomb and he died shortly after.

2) When Tutankhamun's mummy was unwrapped, the archaeologists found a curse wrapped in the bandages. It said: 'They who enter this sacred tomb shall swiftly be visited by the wings of death.'

3) When Lord Carnarvon died, his favourite dog howled and died at the exact moment of his death. The dog was 3,000 miles away in England.

4) A worker in the British Museum was fastening labels to things stolen from Tutankhamun's tomb. He dropped dead shortly after.

5) American millionaire George Gould visited the tomb. He was fine before he went, but died the next day.

6) The mummy's 'curse' is in fact ancient Egyptian germs that were sealed into the tomb 3,000 years ago.

21

AWESOME EGYPTIAN QUIZ

So you think you now know a thing or two about the awesome Egyptians? Test your knowledge with this multiple choice quiz and see if you're a true Egyptian expert or not.

1. What percentage of Egyptians lived as slaves, er, sorry, peasants? (Of course, they might as well have been slaves!)
a) 20%   **b)** 40%   **c)** 90%

2. The pharaoh proved his fitness to be king by doing one of the following trials:
a) killing at least 100 enemies by his own hand within the first five years of his reign
b) running round a gruelling obstacle course after he'd reigned for 30 years
c) having at least four children by the end of the tenth year of his reign

3. Gods played a very important role in Egyptian life. Which of these three is actually an Egyptian god?
a) Re – the Sun God. Some said he made people. The Egyptians called themselves, 'the cattle of Re'.
b) Ta – the Moon God. Egyptians would howl to Ta when the moon was full.
c) Bla – the god of the universe. Egyptians made animal sacrifices to him twice a month.

4. Egyptians spent most of their lives worrying about:
a) taxes   **b)** the plague   **c)** the afterlife

5. The Egyptians who could read and write were called:
a) wordsmiths
b) scribes
c) editors

6. Why did Egyptians make their dead (at least the ones who could afford it) into mummies?
a) to scare away grave robbers
b) bodies that rotted wouldn't make it into the afterlife
c) to keep the rats from nibbling on their toes

7. How many pyramids were built in ancient Egypt?
a) 35   **b)** 96   **c)** 57

8. What happened to certain body parts that were taken out of a dead body?
a) They were put into canopic jars.
b) They were thrown into the River Nile.
c) They were burned at the entrance to the pyramid.

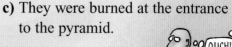

9. What do many people believe happened when you robbed a pharaoh's tomb?
a) The ceiling would collapse on top of you.
b) You would be cursed by the mummy and probably die.
c) Your brain would turn to jelly.

WARNING
AWESOME SPELLS MAY SERIOUSLY DAMAGE YOUR HEALTH

ANSWER PAGES

PAGES 2-3: WHAT IS AN AWESOME EGYPTIAN?

There were few slaves in Egypt…

30 peasants and cattle work on Ali Fayed's land. Remember, women were not counted.

When the Nile was in flood…

Peasant C faces the chop.

Some peasants who worked hard…

Unscrambled words in the correct order: STONE BLOCKS, BURNING DESERT, BREAD, OINTMENT, LIMESTONE, MUD FLOORS, CROWDED, WATER, TOILETS, STUNK, SEWAGE, ANIMALS, STARVATION.

PAGES 4-5: WRITE LIKE AN EGYPTIAN

See if you can read these two…

Pyramids ar(e) big   My nits ar(e) itchy

If you think school is bad…

Unscrambled words in the correct order: IDLE, CURSED, NOT, HEART, PLEASURE, SHALL, SPEND, IDLENESS, BEATEN, BOY'S, BACKSIDE, WHEN, BEATEN!

Can you find the list of these…

1) GIZA
2) SAND
3) CHARM
4) RING
5) INK
6) SPIRITS

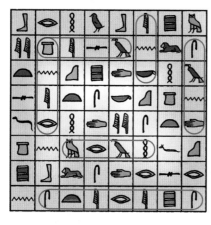

PAGES 6-7: GRUESOME GODS

Egyptian gods were unbelievably…

1 = J   2 = G   3 = K   4 = A   5 = C   6 = H   7 = E
8 = B   9 = L   10 = I   11 = F   12 = D

Need an awesome answer to a powerful problem?

1 = Sobek   2 = Isis   3 = Thoth   4 = Sekhmet   5 = Hathor

Most awesome Egyptian myths…

Unscrambled words in the correct order: JEALOUS, ORGANISED, ANNOUNCED, SEALED, SEARCHED, BURIAL, ANGERED, SCATTERED, WRAPPED.

PAGES 8-9: PHASCINATING PHARAOHS

Pharaohs ruled for almost 3,000 years…

1 = WOMAN   2 = MURDER   3 = WRINKLY   4 = HUNDRED
5 = MAGICIAN   6 = GOOSE   7 = LION   8 = ELEPHANTS
9 = MONEY   10 = GREEK

After ruling for 30 years…

The carvings on all Egyptian…

PAGES 10-11: POWERFUL PYRAMIDS

There are some awesome things…

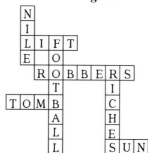

Not everyone agrees the pyramids are…

All except number 3 have been believed by someone.

The biggest pyramid is the…

The word PYRAMID can be seen 6 times in the grid.

PAGES 12-13: POTTY PYRAMIDS

Can you find the words listed in…

The *Awesome Egyptians* lived 5,000 years ago!

Archaeologists in Egypt…

There are 35 overlapping pyramids.

PAGES 14-15: MAGICAL MUMMIES

The men who made dead bodies…

Instructions in the correct order: D, F, J, B, A, E, H, C, I, G.

The following mummies will tell you…

1, 2, 4, 5, 6 & 7 = TRUE   3 = FALSE

PAGES 16-17: FATE OF THE MUMMY

The monsters that live in the Duat…

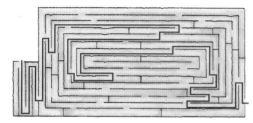

At the gates of Yaru…   *The Egyptians mummified more…*

Pilgrims came to ancient Egypt like…

1 = RABBIT   2 = FISH   3 = DOG   4 = PIG   5 = DUCK
Pilgrims bought mummified CATS as souvenirs.

PAGES 18-19: GRUESOME GRAVE-ROBBERS

Cast yourself back in time…

1 = No. You will need a group of at least 7 or 8 people to help you.
2 = Yes. They will help you to enter the tomb and open the coffin.
3 = No. You should find a back entrance. With the front entrance untouched, no one will suspect anything's wrong.
4 = Yes. You will need the officials and priests to turn a blind eye.
5 = Yes. The gold will be melted down, ready for you to move it easily.
6 = No. Merchants can buy your stolen treasures – no questions asked.
7 = No. Many a grave-robber was caught this way. People wanted to know where all that wealth came from.
8 = No. You need to know the passages and rooms as well as a tomb builder.
9 = Yes. It could save you a lot of trouble.
10 = Yes. You will be tortured and then executed.

Pharaohs eventually realised that…

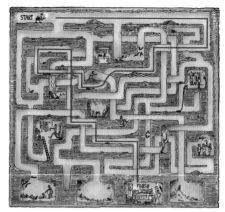

Many tomb-builders became grave-robbers…

PAGES 20-21: CURIOUS CURSES

Lots of 'true' mummy stories have been told…

Story in the correct sequence: G, A, M, H, B, I, C, F, L, N, D, J, K, O, E

Lord Carnarvon ignored his friend's…

The death of Lord Carnarvon was…

1 = True, but… Mace had been ill before he entered the tomb. He had pleurisy. There were no cures for this illness in 1922.
2 = Lies. A newspaper reported this curse soon after Carnarvon's death.
3 = True, but it's a creepy story told by Lord Carnarvon's son.
4 = Lies. The British Museum never had any objects from Tut's tomb.
5 = Mistake. Gould was not in good health before his visit. He went to Egypt because he was ill, but the stress of travelling killed him.
6 = Mistake. The air in the tomb wouldn't be very healthy, but King Tut's germs wouldn't kill a visitor.

PAGE 22: AWESOME EGYPTIAN QUIZ

1 = c   2 = b   3 = a   4 = c   5 = b   6 = b   7 = b   8 = a   9 = b

Scholastic Children's Books,
Commonwealth House, 1–19 New Oxford Street,
London WC1A 1NU, UK
A division of Scholastic Ltd
London ~ New York ~ Toronto ~ Auckland ~
Sydney ~ Mexico City ~ New Delhi ~ Hong Kong
Published in the UK by Scholastic Ltd, 2004
Some of the material in this book has previously
been published in Horrible Histories: *The Awesome
Egyptians* and *The Awesome Ancient Quiz Book*

Text copyright © Terry Deary, 1993, 2001
Illustrations copyright © Martin Brown, 1993–2001
All rights reserved

ISBN 0 439 96293 5

2 4 6 8 10 9 7 5 3 1

The right of Terry Deary and Martin Brown to be
identified as the author and illustrator of this work
respectively has been asserted by them in
accordance with the Copyright, Designs and
Patents Act, 1988.

Additional material by Jenny Siklos
Additional illustrations and colour work by
Stuart Martin

Created and produced by The Complete Works,
St Mary's Road, Royal Leamington Spa,
Warwickshire CV31 1JP, UK

Printed and bound
by Tien Wah Press Pte. Ltd, Singapore